I0003976

ECHO DOT

Settingup Alexa and Echo Dot

BY

STEPHEN C. HAYES

Copyright©2020

COPYRIGHT

TABLE OF CONTENT

CHAPTER 1

INSIDE

The introduction of the Amazon Echo Dot device by Amazon, was an introduction into living a smarter life and having a smarter home. This device has shown over the years to be a very reliable domestic tool and friend, that can listen and speak back with the promise of making life a lot easier and better.

So many persons, especially the very busy and mostly engaged in one activity or the other, have discovered the mind blowing things that the Echo Dot device can do with ease and convenience.

Some people have said that the Echo Dot device is just an E-reader, without knowing that it can be a trusted friend as it can also be a weather forecaster, news update buddy,

alarm reminder and much more of great importance.

This manual brings to you modestly almost all you should know about Amazon Echo Dot device and easy ways to become a smart home manager, explore unknown features of Echo Dot device, how to troubleshoot your device, how to get your device up and running, etc.

Follow the instructions inside attentively and soon you will be taking care of things like a pro.

CHAPTER 2

ABOUT ECHO DOT

The introduction of the Amazon Echo Dot device by Amazon, was an introduction into living a smarter life and having a smarter home. This device has shown over the years to be a very reliable domestic tool and friend, that can listen and speak back with the promise of making life a lot easier and better.

While Amazon has a range of Echo devices, choosing the Echo Dot device is a very wise decision as it is portable and easy to carry.

The Echo Dot went through some upgrading by Amazon almost four (4) years ago, and it's one of the reasons why there're various models, versions or generations of the device.

The process of activating your Echo Dot can be cumbersome sometimes; it's for this reason that this work is provided. if you are confused and need help finding out how, you are at the right place.

Note: Amazon renewed the Echo Dot in fall of 2016. Both generations of Echo Dots have few similarities. Therefore, this guide covers the second generation model; we shall touch some places where they both have their differences.

There are a number of likenesses between the first and second generations of Echo Dot, and in this work we shall be addressing a number of them and more.

Look out for the following:

a. Setting up Echo Dot

b. Primary commands of Alexa and more.

c. Echo Dot necessary functions

d. Alexa App settings adjustment

e. Troubleshoot Echo Dot device

CHAPTER 3

AMAZON ECHO DOT SETUP

Below are some of the things you will find in the Echo Dot box:

→ A working power adapter.

→ Alexa command list cards.

→ The Echo Dot device

→ A USB cable to power the device.

→ Starters setup manual.

Firstly plug in the USB cable from the pack to the Echo Dot. Then plug in the USB end into the adapter which you will plug into electricity through a socket. Make sure the Echo Dot device is at a central position in the room from where it can hear your command. The device has very sensitive and active microphones that easily pick sounds; so no unnecessary words around it.

A blue light shows up whenever Echo Dot is starting. After starting up, allow it some time to complete the start-up process. Alexa will announce "you are ready to get online now" when the orange light comes up.

UTILIZING THE ALEXA APP

You will need your mobile phone or tablet to continue with the setup of your Echo Dot device. Do well to download and install the right Alexa App. This can work on the following:

→ Amazon Alexa is on Android.

→ Amazon Alexa is on iOS.

→ If there are no smart phones close by, use the Alexa web portal.

You should open the Alexa Apppp and sign in your Amazon account or create, if you don't already have any.

After signing in and agreeing to the terms and conditions of the Alexa page, a number of Echo devices will come up for you to choose from. Because your device is Echo Dot, click on it and choose your language preference, after this select the **Connect to Wi-Fi** button. If you have your device still connected to electricity, the light's colour will remain orange. Now select the **Continue** button.

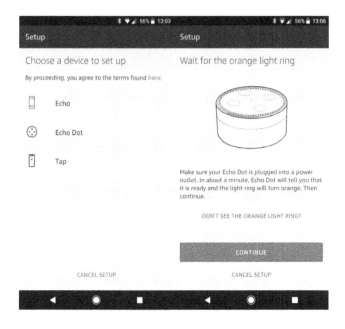

Automatically your mobile phone or tablet will attempt connecting to your Echo Dot. If it doesn't automatically connect, you will be asked to press and hold the Dot's action button (one with a bump) for a couple of seconds. When the device is found, press **Continue** once more.

When you have completed the above, add the Echo to your Wi-Fi network. Your device will be online after you select **Connect.**

Nis you will have to choose from the three options provided for hearing: **Audio Cable, Bluetooth,** and **No Speakers.** These options are to ensure better servicea with audio, as Dots enables connection to your device to a speaker via Bluetooth or an audio cable. Should you not desire any of the above, all audios will be played via the Dots speakers.

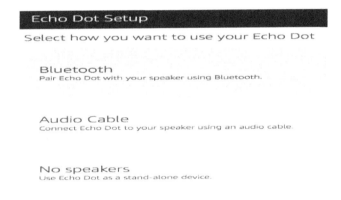

When you have finished the setup, you will be prompted to see a quick video on how to use the Alexa.

CHAPTER 4

ALEXA FUNCTIONS AND COMMANDS

Having completed the setup process, you can start commanding by saying the wake word "**Alexa**" next by a command. Something like "**Alexa, what time is it?**" And your Echo will reply you. Subsequently we shall talk more on the commands, nevertheless keep trying new ones as in worse case Alexa will tell you she doesn't know.

BUILT-IN ALEXA COMMANDS

Below are some samples:

Alexa...

a. **Give me my Flash Briefing:** Echo Dot will read to you latest news headlines and updates. We shall talk about choosing your need source later.

b. **What date is it:** Alexa will tell you what day it is when you lose track.

c. **Switch on the lights:** Alexa can turn on or off the light of you are operating a smart home.

d. **Set alarm for 7am:** You can program an alarm on your Echo without using your clock or phone. You can even fix a schedule by simply saying **Set a repeating alarm for 7am weekdays.**

e. **Track my order:** If you desire to know when your Amazon package will be arriving? Alexa can help.

f. **Set a timer for 5 minutes:** This Alexa will do.

g. **Play the Kenny G station on Pandora:** details on operating music will be given below.

h. **Order for laundry detergent.** Echo makes ordering from Amazon simple.

Just mention the name of the goods you desire to buy (if you are not precise, Alexa will list common options). When you are not certain, send the goods to your Amazon cart instead.

i. **How is the traffic?** If you have your office address in the settings (details in subsequent page), Alexa will tell you your possible commute time.

j. **What restaurants are nearby?** easy job for Alexa.

k. **Stop:** use this general command to end audio playback, or to make Alexa keep quite.

l. **What is the extended forecast for McMurdo Station Antarctica?** If you ask your Echo for weather forecast without being precise, you will be replied using your your current location

m. **Add finish building my PC on my to-do list:** Echo can create a to-do list via Alexa.

n. **Add books to my shopping list:** Here, your device can organize a shopping list for you and help you remember what you need to buy.

You may see more command information in the Alexa App. Select the **Home** button on the screen to see every command you have given to your Echo. If you previously asked Alexa about nearby Chinese restaurants to eat and a few names were provided, still visit the App to see reviews, business hour, and addresses.

If you want to see more command to try on Alexa, there is a part of the App dedicated to this. From the left side menu, you can select **Things to Try** and a list of options will be displayed.

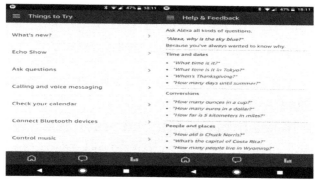

AMAZON ECHO DOT ABILITIES

Echo Dot has much more abilities than I can readily state now, there are numerous skills you can check for and add to it. To see these abilities, open the Alexa App and select "**Ability**" from the left menu.

Here you will find the skills outlined; this at first may seem confusing, but you can always go through and get new skills easily. there will be a number of common demands and then going below, you will find categories such as **Local, Productivity,** and **Health and Fitness.**

You can as well check with the search bar on top.

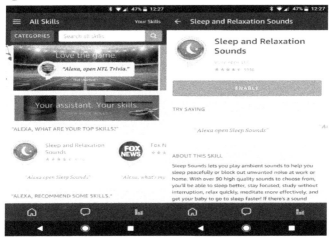

Choose a skill and study it, as everyone has phrases you can ask Alexa. If you are not satisfied still, go through the developers description and see reviews. All you have to do is just select the **Enable Ability** option at the top to include it into your Echo. Then command Alexa to launch it. You can also command Alexa to add skills to your list.

CHAPTER 5

FUNCTIONS OF ECHO DOT

Having finished the setup procedure and now know how and what to ask Alexa. For even more benefits, let's look at more of the amazing Echo Dot functionalities.

LIGHTS & BUTTONS FUNCTION ON ECHO DOT

We can begin now by talking about the various buttons on your Echo Dot device and their functions.

a. **Off/On Microphone Button:** This button is to either turn off or on the Echo Dot microphone. To do this, press down the button. If it shows red color, it means that your Echo Dot microphone has been turned off and can therefore not hear the wake word or your commands.

b. **Action Button:** the action button has a dot on top of the Echo button, it's for starting up your device (same function as the wake word) and ending a ringer alarm or timer.

c. **Plus and Minus Button:** This button controls the volume of the device. The white ring light on the Echo Dot bibs or increases to signify the current volume. If you desire to use voice control, just say **"Alexa, volume five," (**Volume number 1 to 10 will respond). First generation Echo Dot volume can be controlled by rolling the outer ring.

There are some colours relatively common but important in the operations of the Echo Dot that you should know:

a. **Solid Red:** Means the microphone is not working.

b. **Solid Blue with Rotating Cyan Lights:** This light comes up when you are starting up your device. When this happens frequently, check properly as you might be unknowingly unplugging your device.

c. **Pulsing Green Light:** This comes up if there's an unread message or unanswered call.

d. **Solid Blue with Cyan Sliver:** This shows up whenever your Echo Dot is working on your command.

e. **Waves of Violet:** This shows up whenever your device has difficulty or error connecting to Wi-Fi. Check out the subsequent chapter on troubleshooting if this is reoccurring.

f. **Pulsing Yellow Light:** This shows up only when you get a message. Just say **"Alexa, play my message"** to read the message.

g. **All Lights off:** You see this whenever your Echo Dot device is in standby mode.

h. **Flash of Purple Light:** This is a "Do Not Disturb" signal that comes up if Alexa is trying to figure things out.

ADD A MUSIC ACCOUNTS

One of the amazing features of Echo Dot is playing music. With just a command to your Echo Dot device you can have your desired music playing as it suits your mood. This is much more convenient than scrolling through your phone for a music of your choice.

If you prefer streaming music through your device, then you may have to link your accounts to be able to access your library. Simply open the Alexa App and on the left menu, tap "**Settings**" then go down and tap "**Music and Media**." Once on this page you will see all the music apps available; like Amazon Music, iHeartRadio, Pandora, and Spotify. Select your desired music service and go through the process of signing in and then link it to your Echo Dot account.

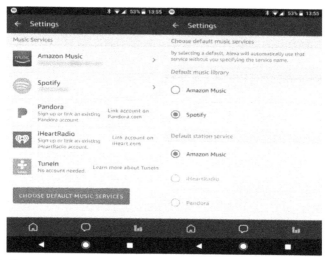

   When you are signed in, it's now left for you
to **Choose Default Music Service** button.
Putting a music service centre as default
makes it your primary music provider. i.e
when you give a command to Alexa, "**Alexa,
play some jazz music**" and Spotify is set as
default, Alexa will only play from Spotify.
Anytime you wish to play through a different
service, add "**from Amazon music**"
anytime you wish to hear music.

VIDEOS AND BOOKS

Move away from the left menu and hit the **Music, Video, and Books** option, and you will find lots of services. Remember we have already talked about music, but Alexa still got a few more tricks hidden.

Beneath the **Video** section, is an option for your Echo to be connected to a Fire TV or Dish Hopper Smart DVR. These allows you to control playback using your voice, which is pretty slick.

If you are more of a book person, move down and you can access your Audible and Kindle libraries on Echo. Alexa can read your Audible audio books, as well as every Kindle eBook you have. They must come from the Kindle store, and Alexa can't read comics or graphic novels. You also won't be able to reduce the reading speed. Despite this, it's a suitable way to meet up on reading even while you are busy working.

GET YOUR ECHO DOT CONNECTED TO EXTERNAL SPEAKERS

Echo Dot has good speakers that works perfectly well for talking to Alexa. While they will not fill the room with so much sound, they get the job done for basic commands. Meanwhile, they are noticeably superb when it comes to playing music. However, you might want to get your Dot connected to an external speaker via Bluetooth or an audio cable for good sound quality.

If you want to use a 3.5mm audio cable, just simply plug one end of the cable into your Echo and then the other end plug into the speakers you want to make use of. Hence, whenever Alexa plays any audio, through the speakers you will hear it. Ensure to put the volume level of both devices at a suitable level, to enable you hear it loud and clear. Note that you won't be able to do reverse and use the cable to play music on your Dot from another device.

If attempting to connect a Bluetooth speaker, go to the settings menu. Open the Alexa App, move to the left menu, and click on **Settings.**

You will see your device listed under the **Devices**. Click on it and select **Bluetooth.**

When the next page opens, click on **Pair a New Device** and put your speaker in Bluetooth pairing mode. Click on your speaker as displayed to connect and your Echo will play all audio through it. Whenever you desire to disable the connection, just command Alexa saying "**Alexa, disconnect Bluetooth**" and your audio will resume playing through your Echo Dot, and to reconnect say **Alexa, connect Bluetooth.** See that your speaker 'on' when carrying out this command.

VOICE CALLS AND MESSAGES

One new impressive feature of the latest Echo Dot device is the ability to make free calls and send free messages to other Echo devices. You can communicate with your pals live for free. Click the **Messaging** option on the App screen to see your messages or send from the App.

Visit our guide for more details on Echo calling.

THE SMART HOME FUNCTIONS

The Echo Dot is a tremendous advancement in setting up a smart home. To do this, click on **Smart Home** option on the App, you will see Echo's hub for adding and tweaking new devices. To set up a isn't part of this book, but you can check it and see if you don't already have any.

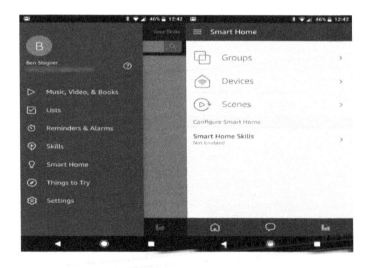

CHAPTER 6

SET UP YOUR ALEXA APP

In the previous pages we have highlighted some of the basic uses of your Echo Dot, Alexa and adding skills. Go through your Alexa App on your mobile device to explore the usefulness of your device. To get it, go to your menu and tap on **Settings**. Below are however, some of the functions within:

CHANGING THE WAKE WORD OF YOUR ECHO DOT

Basically the general Echo devices wake word by default is **Alexa.** This can however be changed to others as you feel convenient, and to do this go to **Settings,** click on the name of your device, then go to **Wake Word.** Choose from any of these, **Alexa, Echo, Computer,** and **Amazon.**

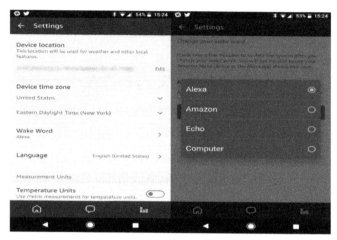

The Star Trek fans should relate to the last one better. Note that changing your wake word you can help keep your device from being hijacked.

PAIRING A REMOTE WITH YOUR ECHO DOT

Scroll to:

→ **Settings**

→ **Device**

→ **Pair device remote,** and sync it this way:

TURNING ON "DO NOT DISTURB"

If you have friends who posses Echo devices and won't rest, go to **Settings**

Device, and once there switch on

"**Do Not Disturb",** and Alexa won't bother you with any call or text. There's also an option of setting a convenient time "Do Not Disturb" activates every day automatically.

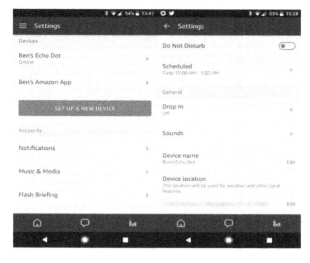

If you don't want to go through your device to do this, just say "**Alexa, switch on/off Do Not Disturb"**

ECHO DOT SOUND OPTIONS

If you are not satisfied with the sound of your Echo Dot, you can go to "**Settings**" and input your device's name, then click "**Sounds**".

Check out a new alarm sound options by going to "**Alarm**" . But make certain you set your **Alarm, Notification Volume, and Timer** in a convenient volume and likewise turn off the "**Audio**" option through "**Notifications**" if you don't want to be distracted.

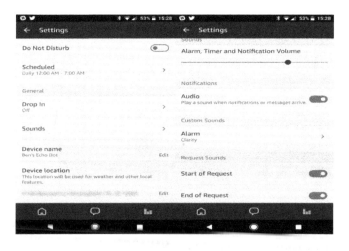

It's necessary to know that Echo has a switch on tune for both the **"Start of Request, and End of Request"**. That's why when you say **Alexa,** your Echo will make that tune to signify you were heard. Same tune will be heard when Echo notices you are done speaking.

CHANGE YOUR ECHO DOT DEVICE LOCATION

Your Echo is programmed to set its location automatically. But in case otherwise, just go to:

"Settings - Device - Device location," then set your present address. This is necessary if you must get correct information about local details.

SHIPPING NOTIFICATIONS ON YOUR ECHO DOT

If you desire to know always, Go to:

"Settings - Notifications - Shopping Notifications"

And turn on the **Shipment Notifications.**

Anytime you see a yellow ring light, ask Alexa to read out your notifications:

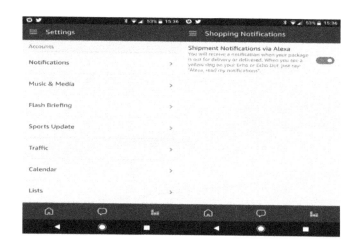

SELECT ECHO DOT NEWS SOURCES

Go to "**Settings - Flash Briefing**" to change your news channels. By default, your news source is NPR's hourly news summary and weather updates. To include sources, click "**Get more Flash Briefing content**" and include your desired news source.

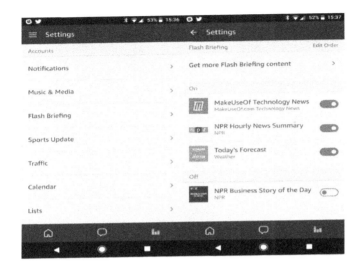

ADD FAVOURITE SPORTS TEAMS ON YOUR ECHO DOT

To achieve this, say **"Alexa, sports update"** and you will be told how your favourite teams are doing and when their next games are. You however need to be specific about which teams you favour for better servicing. To do this, go to **"Settings - Sports Update"** menu.

Search for a team and click add to include new teams to already existing list.

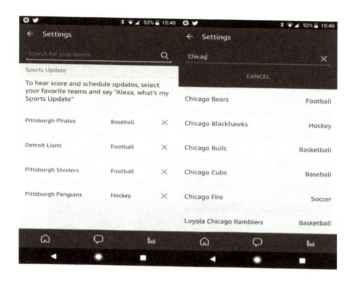

CREATE A WORKPLACE ON YOUR ECHO DOT

Remember we mentioned Alexa's traffic update ability? Go to **"Settings -Traffic"** to specify your daily commute. First put in your "home address" and then the "destination of your work place". If you wish, include a stop along to get a cup of morning coffee, or drop kids off at school.

CONNECT CALENDAR TO ECHO DOT

Alexa can include items to your calendar and notify you of upcoming events daily. To do this, go to "**Settings - Calendar**"

You can choose to connect to Google, iCloud calendars, etc. just choose the one that suites you most thereafter sign into your account to link them.

MAKE A TO-DO LIST WITH YOUR ECHO DOT

Alexa App provides primary to-do list. If you use other service, you should add it by going to, **"Settings - Lists"**

Pickfrom the already known services like Any.do, To-Do list, cozi list, etc. thereafter sign into your accounts and link up your lists.

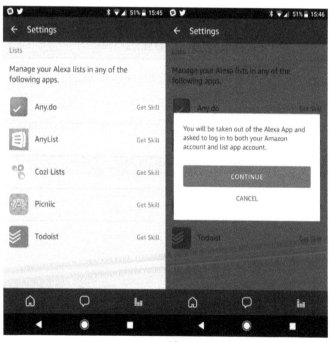

IMPROVE ALEXA

If Alexa starts having difficulty hearing your commands correctly, you can do a quick training session for her. To do this go to **"Settings - Voice Training."** After which attempt reading about twenty-five (25) phrases in your normal voice from a reasonable distance. This will make Alexa know how you sound and recorgnize when you speak.

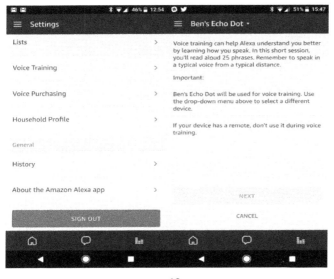

ADD A PIN OR DISABLE THE VOICE PURCHASING ON ECHO

Getting to purchase stuffs on Amazon with just your voice command can be very expensive and tempting. To disable this option therefore, go to **Settings - Voice Purchasing.**

Once here, disable the **Purchase by voice** option or set a four-digit code that will be asked before every voice purchases. This will keep others from buying without your consent.

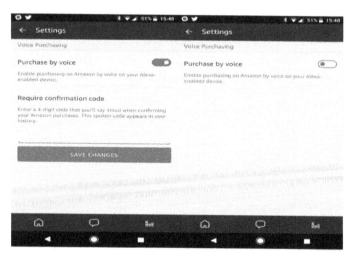

ENABLE MULTIPLE HOUSEHOLD MEMBERS ON YOUR ECHO DOT

To do this go to **Settings - Household Profile,** if you wish to include other user to your Amazon household. This will give both of you equal access to the other contents and allows sharing lists of items and many other features.

CHAPTER 7

SOME TROUBLES WITH ECHO DOT

There are some common reoccurring troubles that you might encounter in the process, and we shall be talking about troubleshooting.

Firstly, it's worthy of note that, as rebooting your personal computer (PC) fixes lots of problems, so it does with Echo Dot. To reboot Echo Dot, unplug it, wait a few seconds, then plug it again and allow it boot completely.

WHEN ALEXA CAN'T HEAR YOU

If you notice Alexa is not responding because she can't hear you, take your Echo Dot far from (at least 9 inches) any obstruction or obstacle.

Now listen and observe for other noise that might make Alexa not to hear you clearly. Some possible noises include Air conditioner working all day where your Echo Dot is or Playing music with volume too high.

WI-FI CONNECTION TROUBLES

One usual issue noticed in setting up Echo Dot is it's difficulty connecting or staying connected to Wi-Fi. If this is the issue, then firstly reboot all your internet devices, including the Dot, modem, and router. If the issue persists, move your router and Echo nearer. See that your Dot is kept far from devices like domestic microwaves, these may be interfering with the device connectivity. Lastly, check and disconnect other dormant devices sharing your network to avoid waste of bandwidth.

ALEXA DOESN'T UNDERSTANDS YOU

When you notice each time you ask Alexa a question you receive a wrong answer, maybe because Alexa doesn't hear properly. Going through a voice training session as earlier stated will take care of this situation. Go to **Settings - Voice Training**

After which attempt reading about twenty-five (25) phrases in your normal voice from a reasonable distance. This will make Alexa know how you sound and recorgnize when you speak.

If this doesn't take care of the issue, go to **"Settings - History"** in there you will see what Alexa heard you command. Click on any of them to play the live audio back and see if Alexa did as you commanded. In doing this try to figure out problem words as it will guide you to speak more clearly.

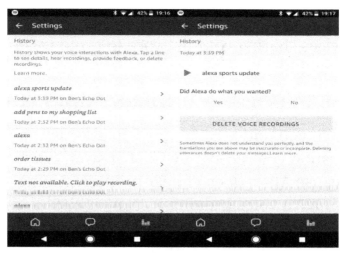

FROZEN?

FACTORY RESET YOUR ECHO DOT

The last resort to any trouble your device might be having, is to do a factory reset and send it back to default settings. This means that all your data and information will be wiped clean and you might need to start all over again.

To factory reset the second generation Echo Dot devices, press and hold the **Microphone off** and **Volume down** button together for about 15 seconds. You will see the light ring go orange and then blue. Which shows your Echo is ready.

On the other hand, the first generation Dot devices have a program reset button with it. Look for the **Reset** button on your device, and use a paper clip to press and hold the button. You will see the light ring go orange and then blue. Which shows your Echo is ready.

THE END

www.ingramcontent.com/pod-product-compliance
Lightning Source LLC
LaVergne TN
LVHW041221050326
832903LV00021B/726